COINS AND MONEY

PENNIES!

LEE FITZGERALD

New York

Published in 2016 by The Rosen Publishing Group, Inc.
29 East 21st Street, New York, NY 10010

First Edition

Editor: Katie Kawa
Book Design: Katelyn Heinle

Photo Credits: Cover, p. 1 (piggy bank) Lizzie Roberts/Ikon Images/Getty Images; cover, pp. 5, 9, 10, 13, 14, 17, 18, 21, 24 (background design element) Paisit Teeraphatsakool/Shutterstock.com; pp. 1, 5, 9, 10, 14, 17, 21, 24 (coins) Courtesy of U.S. Mint; pp. 5, 10, 13, 18, 22 (vector bubbles) Dragan85/Shutterstock.com; p. 6 Mel Yates/The Image Bank/Getty Images; pp. 9, 14, 21 (vector bubble) LAN02/Shutterstock.com; pp. 13, 24 (dollar bill) Fablok/Shutterstock.com; p. 13 (stack of pennies) karen roach/Shutterstock.com; p. 14 (old penny) tab62/Shutterstock.com; p. 17 (Abraham Lincoln) Getty Images/Staff/Getty Images News/Getty Images; pp. 18, 24 (Lincoln Memorial) Jorge Salcedo/Shutterstock.com; p. 18 (Lincoln Memorial penny) mattesimages/Shutterstock.com; p. 22 (boy) mimagephotography/Shutterstock.com; p. 22 (coin stacks) KWJPHOTOART/Shutterstock.com.

Library of Congress Cataloging-in-Publication Data

Fitzgerald, Lee.
  Pennies! / Lee Fitzgerald.
     pages cm. — (Coins and money)
Includes bibliographical references and index.
ISBN 978-1-4994-0729-7 (pbk.)
ISBN 978-1-4994-0726-6 (6 pack)
ISBN 978-1-4994-0502-6 (library binding)
1. Cent—Juvenile literature. 2. Money—United States—Juvenile literature. I. Title.
CJ1836.F58 2016
737.4973—dc23
                                    2014048199

Manufactured in the United States of America

CPSIA Compliance Information: Batch #WS15PK: For Further Information contact Rosen Publishing, New York, New York at 1-800-237-9932

CONTENTS

Pennies are a kind of metal money called coins.

People use pennies and other coins to buy things.

A penny is one cent.
This is written on the back
of the penny.

9

Five pennies are the same as one nickel. They're both five cents.

One **dollar** is the same as 100 cents. One dollar is the same as 100 pennies.

The way the penny looks
has changed over time.

A man's face is on the front of the penny. He is President Abraham Lincoln.

Older pennies have a
building on the back.
It is the **Lincoln Memorial**.

Newer pennies have a **shield** on the back. This stands for the United States.

21

Nate has three nickels. This is the same as how many pennies?

WORDS TO KNOW

dollar

Lincoln Memorial

shield

INDEX

WEBSITES

Due to the changing nature of Internet links, PowerKids Press has developed an online list of websites related to the subject of this book. This site is updated regularly. Please use this link to access the list: www.powerkidslinks.com/cam/pen